LET'S MOVE

Book 3

D0494450

York St. John College

3 8025 00445712 6

LET'S MOVE

Enjoyable Physical Activities and Games
for Children between the Ages of 3 and 7
Book 3

OFF WE GO OUTSIDE!

YORK ST. JOHN
COLLEGE LIBRARY

Meyer & Meyer Sport

Editor: Heidi Lindner, Pipo-Lernwerkstatt, Neumünster
Authors: Gisela Stein, Heidi Lindner
Illustrations: Silke Mehler
Translation coordination: Gisela Stein
Translated by Jean Wanko

Off We Go Outside/ed. by Heidi Lindner
-Oxford: Meyer & Meyer Sport (UK) Ltd., 2002
(Let's Move: 3)
ISBN 1-84126-066-5

All rights reserved, especially the right to copy and distribute,
including the translation rights. No part of this work may be
reproduced – including by photocopy, microfilm or any other means
– processed, storedelectronically, copied or distributed in any form
whatsoever without the written permission of the publisher.

© 2002 by Meyer & Meyer Sport (UK) Ltd.
Aachen, Adelaide, Auckland, Budapest, Graz, Johannesburg,
Miami, Olten (CH), Oxford, Singapore, Toronto
Member of the World
Sports Publishers' Association
www.w-s-p-a.org

Printed in Germany by Druckpunkt Offset GmbH, Bergheim
ISBN 1-84126-066-5
E-Mail: verlag@meyer-meyer-sports.com
www.meyer-meyer-sports.com

Publisher's Statement

The games and exercises described in this book have been tried and tested many times,
without any problems, by the authors and the children in their care. However, teachers,
parents and any other adults using this book for source material must ensure that the
children in their care play within a safe and secure enviroment. The publisher cannot be
held liable should accidents occur. Correct and standard procedures on health and
safety should be followed at all times.

CONTENTS

DEAR READERS,

Do children actually still go outside and play? Or have we reached a point where increased traffic, perceived dangers lurking around every corner and the isolation of children have forced them into arranged playtime with other children mainly in the company of their mothers and older brothers and sisters?

This edition of "LET'S MOVE" offers a wide range of suggestions for using both the immediate and more distant areas around sports halls and nursery schools to get us moving about in the fresh air, to make important and natural discoveries about our bodies and to increase our powers of perception. All of our suggested activities only require brief preparation. In the end it's always the weather that determines whether we go out or stay inside.

We just need to mention one minor restriction at this point concerning the "Fun Activities" – "Woodland detectives", "A house in the woods," and "The long-lost treasure". These require a certain amount of preparation time to make them into a memorable experience for the children and a satisfying activity for the exercise leader. Time and again we've seen that the bright, sparkling eyes of the children more than compensates for all of our hard work.

And so we wish you many positive experiences and memorable events with the children as well as plenty of sunny days where you can say: "Off we go outside!"

Your authoresses: Gisela Stein, Silke Mehler and Heidi Lindner.

FINGER GAMES
AND SONGS

Beetles and spiders are not exactly the most cuddly or impressive woodland dwellers and yet they are extremely fascinating for children.

How often do children draw our attention to a little crawling beetle or a spider, doing gymnastics on its web, whilst we're out for a walk?

So, it's important to include them in this edition of "LET'S MOVE".

THE COURAGEOUS LITTLE BEETLE

It was a beautiful morning about half past seven
when a little beetle set out on his way to heaven.

The fingers of the right hand move slowly,
up the left arm, which is streched up into the air.

A long blade of grass pointed the way
so he set off in a hurry, without any delay.
He didn't have anything better to do that day!

With his six little legs, one step at a time,
he made his way to top, feeling free and fine.

The right hand stops, when it reaches
The fingertips of the left hand.

"Oh, what was that? A dangerous sound
threatening to dump him back to the ground?
How could it be?"

Quick, little beetle, with all your might,
use your six little legs to hold on tight!

Move your left arm with your right arm on the
top of it first gently then fiercely to the left and the right.

A tremendous storm blowed stronger and stronger.
Little beetle could not hold any longer.

Blow hard at your hands.

Ouch! He fell to the ground with a whack-
landing with a thump on his little beetle back.

Let your right hand fall to the ground.

Picking himself up, and shaking himself off,
little beetle decided:
"Ummpphh! For today, that's enough!!!

*Lift your fingers of your right hand and let it
Wiggle on the ground.*

But the whispering wind called softly to him:
"Come, don't give up, it's so nice here.
Pull yourself together, have no fear!"

*Hold your both hands around your mouth,
while whispering the words.*

And the long blade of grass beckoned to him from on high...

"What's fun", said little beetle,
"perhaps I should have another try!"

THE EENTSY, WEENTSY SPIDER

The een-tsy, ween-tsy spi-der climbed up the wa-ter-spout

Down came the rain And washed the spi-der out.

Out came the sun And dried up all the rain. And the

een-tsy, ween-tsy spi-der climbed up the spout a-gain.

The eentsy, weentsy spider climbed up the waterspout.
Down came the rain and washed the spider out.
Out came the sun and dried up all the rain.
And the eentsy, weentsy spider climbed up the spout again.

11

PIECES OF USUAL AND UNUSUAL SMALL APPARATUS

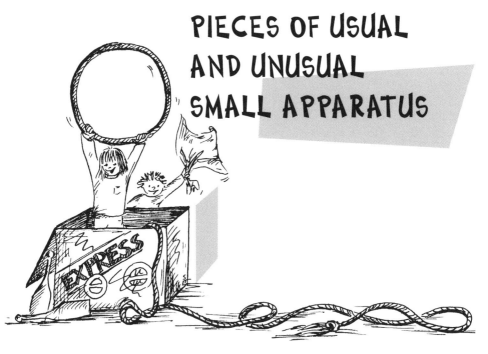

Many unusual pieces of small apparatus have become firm favourites in the equipment stores of our sports halls. However, the everyday materials at the centre of this chapter have such a short "shelf life" that you'll need to keep on renewing them. But, the collecting is fun in its own right and we can happily leave this to the children and their parents.

A lot of brightly coloured autumn leaves are wonderful materials which just ask to be experimented and played with. If there are a few caretakers here and there who can't cope with the idea of having a lot of old leaves in the sports hall, then don't bring them inside, but go and play with them in the woods, especially if you can find a beechwood.

A LOT OF BRIGHTLY COLOURED LEAVES

It's easy to find a large space strewn with leaves either outside or inside. Sometimes it could be difficult to find leaves but yet it is still possible to play these games. You take a stack of news-paper and tear them into leaf-size bits. Of course, leaves would be better.

The children ➡ shuffle through the dry leaves enjoying the noise they make.

The children ➡ shuffle "roads" through the leaves.

The children ➡ take a closer look at some leaves, lift them up above their heads, let them fall through the air and watch where they go.

The children ➡ try to throw handfuls of leaves high up into the air.

The children ➤ throw handfuls of leaves high up into the air and try to catch some of them again.

The children ➤ throw handfuls of leaves to each other and see who can catch some.

The children ➤ let it "rain" leaves.

The children ➤ throw leaves at each other and have a good leaf fight.

The children ➤ shovel the leaves with both hands backwards with legs wide spread.

The children ➥ shuffle and shovel a lot of leaves into various piles and then run a slalom race round them.

The children ➥ jump over the piles of leaves.

The children ➥ jump into the piles of leaves.

The children ➥ lie in the leaves and play roly-poly like tree trunks.

The children ➥ lie on their tummies and let other children cover them with leaves

STORIES TO MOVE TO

·"Stories to move to" take both parents and children off into a fantasy world, where everyone can interpret the individual sections as they wish. Obviously, such stories can be read aloud but it's much nicer and more exciting if they're told freely without a book, because the storyteller can then concentrate more on the actions and contributions the children make, weaving all this into the story. The first story tells of the Bump family and we'll hear all about how they live and some of their big and little adventures. We shall then find out more about exciting things that leaves do in a storm and finally we'll hear about fantastic autumn Kings and their Queens.

OUT WITH THE BUMPS

This story was written for a group, in which Mummy and Daddy play with their children; it can also be played exclusively with children if you omit the parts where parents carry or lift their children.

"One day, I just happened to be out in the woods, sitting high up in a big tree, which stood on the edge of a clearing. And guess what? I could hardly believe my eyes when I saw these little chaps coming towards me. But before I tell you any more, let's build a forest together."

Parents and children or all children ▬ build a fantasy-forest out of little boxes, big boxes, gym horses and anything else they can find.

Exercise leader ▬ sits in a "tree" and carries on with the story.

"Yes, in just such a forest, outside in the country, somewhere in between the dark woods and green meadows, you'll find these wonderful teeny weeny little creatures.

They are only half as big as the nail on my little finger and belong to the Bump family. They are incredibly shy and are terribly afraid of all creatures who are just a little bit bigger than they are.

That's why very few people have seen them until now but, guess what? I've actually been able to watch a little group of them. They'd all arranged to come to a big party for all the "Bump" friends and relations whom they hadn't seen for a year. The Bumps have a cute little habit of always walking in line behind each other when they're on woodland paths and never beside each other."

Parents and children or all children – *walk in a long snake-like line round all the various obstacles in the hall.*

"While they're marching along, they keep on putting their ears to the ground to listen out for any enemies approaching."

Parents and children or all children – *put their ears to the ground and listen.*

"Oh dear, oh dear, I can hear some loud trampling; perhaps it's a deer or a fox. The Bumps all disappear behind trees and bushes, lie flat on the ground or fold themselves up into little parcels."

Parents and children or all children ➡ try to hide behind the apparatus.

"Some Bumps wanted to climb a tree."

Children ➡   *try to climb onto the apparatus.*

"But they don't all manage that. Some of them slide down the tree trunk and bump onto the ground."

Children ➡   *slide slowly onto the ground falling onto their seats.*

"The Bump mummies and daddies are always worried about their children. They quickly lift them up into the air and put them back gently onto their feet."

Parents ▬ *take hold of their children under their arms and lift them up into the air.*

"Hey – that's a great game for the Bump children and they can't get enough of it. Again and again they fly into the air and land on their feet. Some Bump parents even let their children fly around in a circle."

Parents ▬ *lift their children up and spin them around.*

"Then the little creatures remember that they wanted to escape from an enemy, and they have another good listen for danger to see whether or not they might still be found."

Parents and children or all children ▬ *put their right and then their left ear to the ground and listen.*

"All's quiet; perhaps the enemy's lost the scent. So, we can continue our march through the woods, but a bit faster than before."

Parents and children or all children in pairs –   *run behind each other round the room looking for ways of getting around the apparatus.*

"Finally, they all reach the clearing and say 'hello' to each other. There are lots of different ways of doing that, so what do you think might have happened?"

Parents and children or all children –   *invent all sorts of ways of saying 'hello', e.g. with their bottoms, their noses, the tips of their toes, poking each other's belly buttons, etc.!*

"After they've calmed down a bit from the excitement of seeing each other, they talk about all their dangerous experiences of the past year, and what they've learnt from them."

"I," said Billy Bump, "saw a fox last winter, just in time before he could get me. You can imagine how fast I ran away! I only just managed to escape and so now I practise every day with my mummy how to escape from an enemy."

Parents and children or all children –   *all the children run away fast from their parents or partners who then try to catch them.*

"Yes, I can tell a story like that as well," said little Laura Bump. "I'd lost my way in the woods and didn't know how to get out, but fortunately my daddy went looking for me and then found me. Now, let's practise hide-and-seek."

Children –   *hide behind the apparatus and the parents or their partners look for them.*

23

"But what can we do if we need to hide and there's nowhere to hide ourselves?" said little Micky. "Then we'll have to make ourselves as small as we possibly can," Billy Bump suggested.

Parents and children or all children – wriggle along the ground like little dwarts, or crawl on all fours or roll along sideways.

"Do you know what happened to us?" said Merlin. "My brothers and I got caught in a shower of freezing cold rain and there was absolutely nowhere for us to take shelter. You can guess how freezing cold we were and we shivered from head to toe."

Parents and children or all children – hold their hands above their heads as protection, wipe the rainwater off their bodies and stand shivering

"And do you know how we got warm again? We jumped up and down all over the place waving our arms and legs about."

Parents and children or all children –   practise running and hopping, jumping with their legs together, letting their arms and legs fly through the air or jumping about like a Jack-in-a-box.

"Talking about hopping," said Benny, "that reminds me of my adventure. I was walking happily through our forest, when all of a sudden I got stuck in a tree root and sprained my foot. It really hurt and I could only hop on one leg. I'd advice you to practise, just in case you ever need to."

Parents and children or all children –   practise hopping on one leg.

"Now don't laugh at what happened to me next. There was a loud bump, I stretched and stretched myself, opened my eyes and discovered I'd fallen out of the tree, and the whole story about meeting the Bumps in the woods was just one big dream.

But believe me, these teeny weeny creatures exist somewhere and maybe you'll find them one of these days!"

A GIGANTIC TREE TELLS ITS STORY

Everyone hears, plays and experiences together the ever new and exciting adventures of a gigantic tree. Each child first imagines that he/she is a leaf hanging on a beautiful big tree. At the places ".....", please pause for the players' comments or appropriate actions.

A gigantic tree tells the following story (teacher, group leader or child):

"Once upon a time, I had so many leaves hanging at the huge top of my tree that I could hardly hold them all."

The children spread out and hold onto trees or sports hall walls using their hands as stems and act out the story using their own imagination and ideas.

"They waved about happily in the gentle autumn breeze. Little gusts of wind enjoyed rocking the twigs and tickling each leaf. But, as the days went by, the wind got stronger and pulled harder at the leaf stalks, so that they rustled about to the left and the right, and some moved up and down."

Without letting go, the children try to copy the movements.

"The mighty wind blew even harder and my leaves got weaker on the twigs. The wind blew, and blew and blew...."

Everyone blows hard together.

"...Soon the first little stalks came off my twigs, then the medium sized leaves and then, after just one or two more gusts of wind, all the leaves swirled round and round, flying up into the air in every direction. Then they swirled round in circles-...."

Everyone lets go and flies, sails and circles in and out of each other.

"...They then look for their other leafy friends and try to pair up. Then they hop and dance together...."

Several leaves (children) find each other.

".... But then, the wind seems to have gathered renewed strength and blows so hard amongst them that all the leaves fly apart again. Each leaf is blown backwards and forwards...."

Everyone struggles back and forth against the wind.

".... Suddenly, the wind began to play with them and swirled all the leaves into one big circle....,.... then let them all blow one after another around the circle...,"

".... Blew them like a whirlwind into a tight spiral...and then blew them all apart again...."

".... After which they hopped along the ground.... They hopped once, twice, three, four, five times from one place to another...."

Everyone hops about with their feet together, or on one leg or on all fours.

".... And then finally they all land exhausted in a heap on the floor. Only a few little leaves roll along the ground a bit further...."

".... Everyone thought: "That's it!" But wait – something else happened...."

What happened next? Only the gigantic tree in your group knows the answer.

How could you vary this story, if the gigantic tree was a chestnut tree and chestnuts fell down as well?

THE AUTUMN KINGS

This is a story to move to, best done outside. Why don't you go for a walk on a nice, sunny autumn afternoon, (preferably with no wind) into a nearby forest or park and enter the fantastic moving world of nature?

Then, you can tell and enact the following story:

Four autumn kings and queens live happily together in a castle. (e.g. the Leaf King, the Chestnut Queen, the Acorn Queen and the King of the Twigs; or, they could all be Leaf Kings or totally different characters). Every year, they make sure that their park around the castle is cleared up in time for winter, and that they themselves put on their winter decorations. The path through the woods isn't easy and a lot of the castle "citizens" help them with this work.

First, the group of children citizens needs to build a castle courtyard out of all the leaves, twigs and fruits, which they can find in the meadow, on the playground or in the field.

An overgrown path winds its way in a spiral out of the courtyard and into the castle grounds. This path should be wide enough for a child to be able to kneel across it.

Once everything is ready, the children choose 4 kings and queens and they are then sat, knelt or settled in the courtyard.

At this stage, all the citizens start clearing up, going along the path, collecting autumnal materials and bringing them back along the path. However, they need to observe the following royal rules:

Anyone coming back empty-handed from the courtyard and who meets a heavily-laden citizen, drops to their knees. The person carrying autumnal materials climbs over the kneeling child and both then continue on their way.

Once back in the courtyard, the kings are decorated bit by bit with all the autumnal materials. The kings are dressed in new winter crowns and winter clothes using the beautiful brightly-coloured leaves, the shining horse chestnuts, etc. Be careful how you decorate their heads, backs, tummies, etc., so that the kings keep still and nothing falls down.

If a king loses his autumnal decorations, then he chooses another child as king and becomes a citizen.

GAME IDEA 1:
All sorts of materials are gathered from all around, and everyone can take as much as they can carry.

GAME IDEA 2:
Each castle citizen may only take one leaf, one fruit or one twig at a time. The materials are taken straight from the pre-determined end of the path. The game ends this time when all the materials from the path have been used up in the courtyard.

GAME IDEA 3:
The materials are brought into the courtyard with varying accompanying tasks. E.g., going backwards, crawling on all fours, limping or in pairs like a wheelbarrow, etc.

The group itself decides when the game should end, e.g. when the castle grounds have been tidied up, when all the materials have been used up or when it's simply not fun anymore.

LARGE APPARATUS–
MOVING SCENERY

Once a group has been able to experience playing together in the fresh air, and its members have run about in the woods, walked across meadows and fields and maybe even jumped across a little stream, the children subconsciously grasp the connection between the demand made on them by rough ground and their own body skills, especially their sense of balance. By using the large apparatus in the sports hall, it is possible to build on some features in the world of nature and thus enable them to extend their experience.

A BALANCING GARDEN IN THE GYM

On the one hand, it's a time-consuming activity setting up an apparatus course with the children, but it can also be very interesting. As they come with their own ideas, they can plan and fantasize, make and dismiss suggestions. No matter how utopian an idea may seem, it is tested for suitability, while it is being set up so that it either has to be altered or rejected if found to be impractical. That is how the children gain experience, which would not possible if the adults just put a pile of apparatus in front of them.

This method makes the assumption that the group of children has reached school age and that they already have some experience of setting up and taking down large apparatus and moving scenery by themselves in small groups.

As you try out this method, you will see that it is better to begin with a fairly small structure to which small pieces of apparatus can be added. Later, when the children are a bit more experienced, you can move onto something more complicated.

The exercise leader should ensure that there are a few everyday materials available in the sports hall alongside all the other apparatus, e.g. party plates, carpet squares, biscuit tins, etc.

WE THEN PROCEED AS FOLLOWS! —

First of all, the exercise leader prepares his/her group for the task ahead:

"Actually, we really wanted an exciting day to practise all sorts of unknown and fun things, but what have we got in front of us? Nothing but an empty sports hall with absolutely nothing interesting or exciting to do.

What can we do?

Either we can go straight back home again or we can build our own stages for finding out and testing things.

What do you think of that idea?
Do you want to do some building?

Good, then let's have a thought together what we'll need in our "Balancing Garden".

The best way of doing this is to collect and draw all of our ideas on a big sheet of paper. Large rolls of waste paper or old wall paper are needed here with enough wax crayons, felt pens and coloured pencils."

And so a plan is made of a balancing course to cover most of the gym floor.

Now we must see how we can put all our ideas into action and whether we've got enough apparatus for what we want to do. The children then set up their balancing course following their own sketches. They can divide into groups, maybe colour-coded, for this and then all the large apparatus is finally set up safely around the hall.

REMINDER:
The leader must check everything before the children use it.

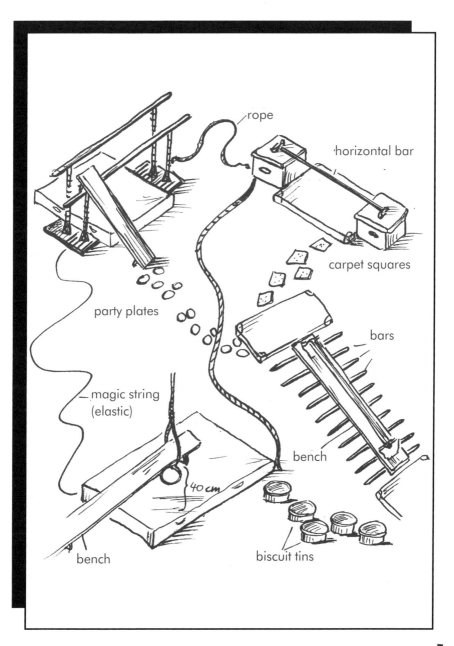

rope

horizontal bar

carpet squares

party plates

bars

magic string
(elastic)

bench

40 cm

bench

biscuit tins

Each group should have the following materials necessary to join all the apparatus together: ropes, party plates, carpet squares, newspapers, etc.

What other everyday materials could help put ideas into practice? Maybe stones, instead of biscuit tins, for example?

Once the course is complete, the children can go around it as they wish, learning to consider each other and not get in other people's way.

When everyone has mastered the setting-up of his/her kind of course, other materials like bean bags, sponge frisbees, paper plates with a tower of building bricks on top, or lids with tennis balls on them can all be carried around the course creating more challenging ways to move.

SMALL GAMES

Small games are indispensable for something to do spontaneously without much preparation. You don't need any special play area, you can manage with a minimum of materials, group size is flexible, and you can adjust the rules of the game to suit both the age and the cognitive ability of the children as well as their physical and motor skills.

EXPLAINING THE RULES

When playing with children outside, give yourself plenty of time to explain all the rules calmly, even if these are very simple in structure for this age group.

To make sure that the children listen, call them together and get them to sit down/or stand quietly.

Eye contact with each child is important to make sure the children both listen and have understood what you say. Once you have all the children looking at you, you can begin to discuss the new game.

You will find the children understand best if you speak to them clearly in short, simple sentences.

You can finish with any questions about things not quite understood.

When all the children have fully understood how the game works, groups are formed and equipment handed out.

The instructions should follow a similar pattern for each game.

"Seek and Run" Happy Families

EQUIPMENT: one bought or home-made Happy Families game (e.g. "Old maid"), several for large groups.

GAME IDEA:

One usually plays Happy Families around a table. The cards are dealt out and taken in turn from the hand of one's neighbour until you have four of the same kind. But who said we have to stay sitting quietly around the table to play this game?

Let's move about; we need to hide the cards in the bushes and trees of a given area and then go looking for them.

PREPARATION:

The exercise leader decides in advance on the number of Happy Families games and whether each child should look for one family or whether the children should go out in pairs or small groups.

The territory is marked out with bright strips of crêpe paper or red and white marker tape before the game starts. The age of the children will determine the size of the territory, but it shouldn't be too small so that the children can reach their maximum endurance potential.

How the game works:

The exercise leader keeps one card from each set of four and mixes up the rest. The shuffled cards are dealt evenly amongst the children (pairs or groups), i.e. the children draw the cards so that they can go and hide them straight away somewhere within the play area. When all the children have come back to the exercise leader, one card is drawn.

Then, the object of the game is to disperse as fast as possible and find all the matching cards.

When all the cards are back with the exercise leader and sorted out, they're shuffled again and the game is repeated.

LITTLE ROLLING BALL

EQUIPMENT: One or two large soft balls.

GAME IDEA:

One child stands inside a circle and must try to get out of the way of a ball being rolled or thrown towards him/her. If hit by the ball, he/she swaps places with the child who threw the ball.

HOW THE GAME WORKS:

Depending on the size of the group, a circle is drawn on the ground with a piece of chalk or a stick.

All the children spread out on the line around the circle with their legs apart and their backs towards the middle, facing outwards.

One child stands in the middle, and must keep out of the way of the ball being rolled or thrown through the legs of the other children around the circle. If the middle child is hit, then the one who threw the ball comes into the middle.

Variation: a second or third ball is brought into the game making escaping being hit more difficult.

DRIVING THE BALL

EQUIPMENT: One volleyball or softball

GAME IDEA:

Who can drive the opposing team over the line? It first looks as if Team A is way out in the lead before coming close to defeat by Team B. It is important to ensure that the children employ clever tactics, i.e. by not all standing in the front line hoping to get the ball, but also defending the rear. The children should learn this by themselves.

HOW THE GAME WORKS:

Two teams are drawn up who stand at throwing distance from each other. Each team fixes a boundary line about 10 metres behind themselves beyond which that team may not be driven.

One player in a team gets the ball and then throws it as far as he can towards the opposing team. The players in that team try and catch or stop the ball in front of their line.

If the ball was immediately caught the current throwing player may take 3 steps forwards. If the ball was merely stopped, then another throw is permitted from where the ball stopped.

Throwing it back aims to drive the other team behind their line. If one team succeeds in driving an opponent behind the rear line, they get a point. Which team has the strongest throwers?

THE HOPPING WAVE

EQUIPMENT: A quoit attached to a piece of rope.

GAME IDEA:

Hey, this game is an extension of the wave which one often sees at sporting events. Standing up at the right place and flinging your arms into the air is childs-play compared with this hopping variation.

HOW THE GAME WORKS:

A quoit knotted to a rope is swung horizontally across the floor in a circle by a child or the exercise leader. All the players stand on the line of the circle in such a way that they have to hop into the air when the ring passes by.

For practising purposes, the rope is kept a bit shorter to begin with, so that the quoit passes in front of the children's feet, but they can already get an idea of the hopping rhythm. Bit by bit, more of the rope can be let out. A child who doesn't jump high enough three times in a row and thus stops the ring swaps places with the middle player.

Who's Got the Stone?

EQUIPMENT: a small stone

Preparation:

All the players stand next to each other in a line. About 15 metres away from this line, a goal line is drawn across the floor.

How the Game Works:

This calls for quick reactions! All the players stand behind each other in a line and fold their hands across in front of their bodies to make a small vessel.

One child has hidden a stone in his/her hand and goes from one child to the next, putting his/her hands each time over the other child's hands, so that nobody knows whether the stone was dropped or not. If a child feels the stone in his/her hands, he/she runs to the finishing line. The rest of the players try to stop that child getting there.

FINISH

THE TREE GHOST

EQUIPMENT: Little stones or clods of earth, a sizeable branch and a long piece of string.

GAME IDEA:

Now and again you'll meet weird things in the woods, I'm sure we've never ever seen something like the tree ghost whom we'll meet today. He looks like the very long branch of a tree with twigs and a lot of grass wrapped around him and he lives in an old tree, where he rocks backwards and forwards on a rope with his head hanging down. This rope isn't just knotted around the tree but lies across one of the lower branches so that you can pull the tree ghost up and down with the bit of spare rope.

HOW THE GAME WORKS:

One child holds the end of the rope and pulls the tree ghost up into the air and then right back down again. All the other children try and hit him with their little stones or clods of earth, and the first one to hit him 3 times can hold the rope. Make sure that all the children throw from the same side, so that nobody gets hurt by the flying missiles.

THE OWL'S AWAKE

EQUIPMENT: A lot of little sticks and/or pine cones which have been collected outside, a plant spray bottle full of water.

GAME IDEA:

Owls can't see during the daytime because their eyes are made to catch their prey at night. So they have to rely on their hearing in particular during the day so that none of their prey is stolen by other animals.

HOW THE GAME WORKS:

All the children go and look for short sticks or pine cones. A circle with a diameter of about 6-8 metres is drawn and the "owl" child stands in the middle. He/she is blindfolded and is given a plant spray bottle full of water, which can be squirted 5 times. All of the little sticks or pine cones are put around the owl, and the other children spread out around the circle, keeping dead quiet and not moving an inch.

The exercise leader chooses 3-4 predatory animals, who must now try to get some of the owl's supplies. They creep in a line towards the prey, whilst the owl tries to guess where they are and drives them away with a water jet. The little predators who have been hit must crouch down and not move until this part of the game is over, i.e. until the owl has squirted water 5 times. Then a new owl is chosen.

A Fox's Walk

Game Idea:

All is not always sweetness and light in the animal kingdom and animals often hunt other animals to eat them in their fight against hunger. We'll show you in our next game how little animals protect themselves from bigger ones. Each child knows that foxes hunt all sorts of little animals, e.g. hares. The children (hares) have build a nest where they can escape to when in danger. You just need a stick to mark out the edge of the nest

How the Game Works:

One child plays the fox and all the others are hares. To start with, the fox moves about amongst the hares' nests without taking any notice of them. The hares hop bravely out of their nests and ask: "Hey, Mr. Fox, what time is it?" "Half past nine," comes the bored answer from the fox.

He continues creeping around and again the hares ask: "Hey, Mr. Fox, what time is it?" "It's quarter to four,".... and the hares continue hopping about. But, if the fox suddenly replies: "Time for dinner!", then the hares have barely enough time to escape back into their nests.

If a hare is caught trying to escape, then he/she becomes the next fox.

THE FOX IN HIS HOLE

GAME IDEA:

We already know from the old song "The fox he would a-wooing go" that foxes like catching geese, and that's just what we want to do in our next game.

HOW THE GAME WORKS:

One child plays the fox, and that fox draws a circle on the ground with a little stick or the heel of a shoe. The circle should be about 2 metres across in which the child sits down.

All the other children are geese who tease the fox: "Hello, Mr. Fox, aren't you hungry today? Wouldn't you like to catch us?" The geese jump in and out of his circle just to taunt him.

But, watch out! Anyone who gets gobbled up (tapped) by the fox, also becomes a fox straight away and helps with the catching.

RABBIT HUNTING

GAME IDEA:

In autumn of every year the hunters gather for a dawn hunt. It's important that all the rabbits hide away so they survive, and so they need a little rabbit warren where they can snuggle down and keep safe.

HOW THE GAME WORKS:

Apart from the two children who are going to be the hunters, all the other players are rabbits. They spread out in a pre-marked area of about 3-4 metres diameter.

It is possible to vary the size of this area depending on your number of rabbits. The rabbits crouch down where they want to stay and draw a circle around themselves, which acts as their burrow, and which they're not allowed to leave.

Both hunters then try and work out the exact position of the burrows, after which they are blindfolded. They must then try and find the rabbits and tap as many of them as possible. The rabbits may move about in their circles, duck down, lie flat on the ground or hide away in the farthest corner of their burrows; but they mustn't come out.

The game ends when the hunters sit down exhausted on the ground.

WAKE UP, YOU BEARS!

GAME IDEA:

There are two bear families living in the forest, Family Grizzlybear and Family Cuddlybear. The Grizzlybears still haven't finished hibernating, which doesn't suit the Cuddlybears, because they want to have a fun party with them. What should they do?

HOW THE GAME WORKS:

The Grizzlybears are lying on the ground asleep and must be woken up. That's not normally difficult to do, but each Grizzlybear has a secret waking-up point, and only when this special point is touched, will he wake up.

Is it his nose?

Under his paws?

Behind his ears?

How long do you think
it will take to wake up
all the Grizzlybears?
Perhaps, afterwards, the Cuddlybears will all hibernate?

What is the best way to wake them up?

Index Card Game Outside

We have a lot of different things to do in our index-card box, all well-suited to making an outside gymnastics session into an intensive moving adventure. In the summer, we get out of the sticky sports hall atmosphere into the playground or local recreation ground or sports field. We can easily pack a bit of equipment and come up with a few rules to ensure that everyone has a good time.

The index-cards are written beforehand and put into a little box. We'll just give you a few examples to get you going, but you can obviously adapt or extend them to suit your own surroundings. It's a good idea to have an equipment list alongside your cards to save time if you're in a hurry.

Equipment List

- 2-4 rounders balls
- several cones
- 2-4 make-up pens
- a game of bowls
- a hard-boiled or plastic egg
- a spoon
- 2 gymnastic rings
- several pieces of chalk
- 2-4 balls
- 2 ropes

We'll quickly explain how the game works:

All the necessary equipment is laid out on the ground.

The exercise leader or teacher stands in the middle and looks after the index-card box.

Working in pairs, the children come to the box and take a card. The exercise leader reads the text, which the children then go and carry out.

Meanwhile, the next pair is ready to perform and so on until all the cards are gone.

Suggestions for possible tasks:

Throw a rounders ball from an agreed line at the wall of a house, a tree trunk or another obstacle.

Do a slalom run around some cones; each of you runs there and back 5 times.

Stand in the middle of the playground and sing a nice song at the top of your voices.

copy model

Find a make-up pen and paint a spot on everyone else's nose.

Find some bowls, a suitable goal and mark out a starting line. Then each of you can try and roll his/her bowls as close to the goal as possible!

Find five things in different shades of green from all around and bring them back here.

5 GREEN

Each of you runs with an egg on a spoon, racing against each other from one side of the playground to the other.

Drive a gymnastic ring across the area. You must keep it rolling with the palm of your hand.

Stand next to each other and hop forwards on one leg. Who can keep going longest?

copy model

Each of you looks for a little bit of wood and draws a nice picture in the sand (assuming you have a sandpit available!), e.g. a house, car or train.

Jog half-way around the sports ground; or perhaps you could manage a whole lap?

Find yourself a big ball and go to the cones; then take turns rolling the ball slalom-style around the obstacles.

copy model

Stand opposite each other and do as many jumping Jacks as you can. Who runs out of breath first?

Each look for two things you can make a noise with.

How many of you here have a birthday in January, February or March? Ask each other.

copy model

Try to find out who's got the biggest feet.

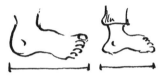

Standing next to each other, jump forwards with your feet together 3 times, but taking each jump in turns. Who lands where?

One of you takes a rope and runs across the playground whilst the other tries to catch the end of the rope. After a short break you can switch places.

copy model

After the end of the session, all the equipment is collected in again and the index cards kept for another sunny day. After we've sung a song together we say "goodbye" and then the children may go home.

The Good Old Street Games — Rediscovered and Fun to Play

Hopscotch and marbles are not exactly the trendiest sort of games but they really don't deserve to be forgotten altogether. Their attraction is that they can be played almost anywhere without any lengthy preparation or hassle. You just need a piece of chalk for flat ground or a little stick for uneven ground to draw your play area, which is done in no time. Also, you can draw hopscotch squares on the sports hall floor or use sticky tape, and then familiarize yourself with the rules.

Hopscotch

Heaven and Hell:

The first child throws a little stone into the square marked "earth" and then hops across all the squares without touching the "hell" square. On the way back he/she picks up the stone from the "earth" square again and jumps out of the hopscotch area. Then the same child throws his/her stone into square 1, hops off after it, but doesn't pick it up again until the return journey. The same procedure is followed until "Heaven" is reached, obviously omitting "hell".

	HEAVEN	
4	HELL	5
	3	
	2	
	1	
	EARTH	

If a child makes a mistake on the way, e.g. throws a stone onto a line, into the wrong square or touches a line with his/her foot, then he/she is "out" for a while. When it is his/her turn again, he/she starts where the mistake was made.

In other variations on the same game, how you move as well as how the stone is thrown can be varied, e.g. hopping with jumps at the end, walking with legs crossed or backwards, or with eyes closed, throwing the stone backwards over your shoulder....

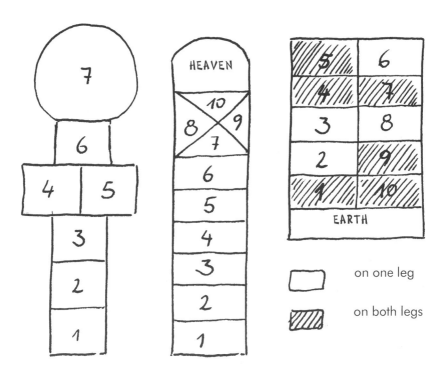

on one leg

on both legs

HOPPING IN A CIRCLE

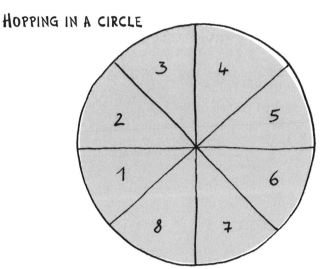

A circle with a 2 metre diameter is drawn on the floor and divided into 8 sections with 4 lines.

The first player then hops into a segment of their choice (e.g. 8) with both feet. From then onwards, they can hop on their left foot into the next segment to the right (7) and with both feet into the next segment, but one to the left (1). Carry on like this, always hopping on one foot to the right then with both feet 2 segments to the left. Anyone touching a line or making a mistake is replaced by the next player. Who can hop all the way round first?

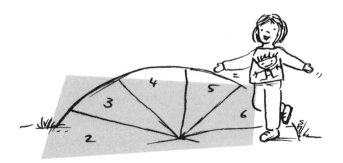

A SNAKE GAME

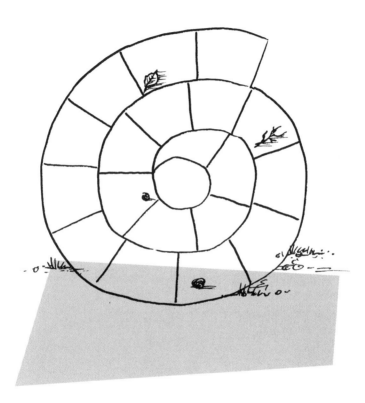

A large snake is drawn on the floor. The coil of the snake is divided into equal sections, which must be big enough for a foot.

The first player hops to the middle on one leg and if he manages it without treading on a line, he can put his own special mark on any one section. The following players can't hop onto that section. If a player goes around twice, he can have a rest on his "own" square. The more sections are "occupied", the harder the hopping becomes.

GAMES WITH MARBLES

It's true that you still find marbles on sale in the shops and they're not expensive, but – where do you still see children playing marbles? Probably all the old rules have gone missing. It's actually a great pity that all sorts of older, traditional games have been forgotten about, maybe irretrievably. If we asked our children to have a look through their toy cupboards and see if they could find some marbles, I'm sure we'd have enough of them to try some marble games with small groups.

THE LUCKY STONE

As many players as possible, a stone, marbles.

There's a stone about the size of an apple lying in the middle of our circle drawn on the ground (about 3-4 metres in diameter). Sitting or kneeling at the edge of the circle, all the players try in turn to roll their marbles at the lucky stone. He/she whose marble ends up nearest to the stone gets all the other marbles in the circle and a new round begins.

BUMPING

2 players, marbles.

They decide who starts. Then the first player takes a marble and rolls it a few metres from the starting line. The second player must bump the first marble with his own and, if he does it, he's won it and a new game begins. But if he doesn't succeed, then the first player takes his marble and tries to hit the other player's marble. Then, if that doesn't work, the game ends in a draw and they start again.

Several players:

There is no "draw" game if several children are playing. If one player doesn't hit the first marble, then both marbles stay where they are, and the next player has a choice of two which he can hit. If he manages to hit one of them, that's his and he can still try to hit the other one. If he doesn't succeed, there are then three marbles to choose from.

Once all the marbles have been hit, a new game can begin.

Tapping

At least 2 players, marbles.

Before play commences, a little hollow is made in the ground and a starting line marked out about 2-3 metres away. Then the order of the players is worked out and the game begins:

Each player now tries to roll a marble into the hollow. The one who manages it first is allowed to tap the other player's rolled marbles into the hollow by pushing them with a bent forefinger.

If he taps the marble past, then it's the next player's turn, who managed to roll a marble into the hollow or, alternatively the one whose marble ended up closest to the hollow.

The winner is the one who rolled the last marble into the hollow and he gets all of them.

FUN ACTIVITIES

If
you were to look up the
word "hike" in a dictionary, you
would find the following definition:
hike ➜ to walk energetically across open
countryside. This is just the right expression to
describe a child's feelings if he or she is asked to go on
a long walk! Children find serious walking stupid, boring,
and loathsome. They don't want to trek off for miles on end
along country footpaths; they want to rustle through leaves,
run down slopes, do some mountaineering, discover things,
follow trails, both to meander and race along; to sum-up all
that: they're looking for adventures and they want to play.
So, if we want to give children a closer experience of the
woods, we need to think up something special, e.g. a
treasure hunt, building a house in the woods or
passing a woodland detective's
examination.

THE FOREST AS A PLACE FOR MOVING AROUND AND EXPERIENCING THINGS

When children come into close contact with nature, they learn to experience important things in quite a unique way, which we can no longer take for granted in today's world. All the various sensual influences must be carefully sought out, planned and introduced to them so that they don't go unnoticed, and this is where exercise leaders and teachers play an important role.

Woods, meadows, unexplored areas with hills, stones, ditches and plants are always an ideal natural playground for children. All their senses and physical skills are called upon here. They can jump over ditches, try to cross little ravines by using branches and tree trunks, climb hills and trees, collect stones, pinecones and acorns, build things with all these materials as well as playing hide-and-seek behind trees and bushes.

Whilst doing this, they have to learn to come to terms with the laws of nature, and both adapt and exert themselves thus making genuinely important discoveries about themselves and their surroundings. Children see themselves as part of a living world in which they too have a place, which they can influence and alter and which, in its turn influences them and requires them to do something.

But – is this natural adventure playground still used?

How often can children play in the woods and go on a voyage of discovery?

We notice time and again that most children today

- hardly know the immediate area in which they live.

- have an excess of perfect toys.

- hardly know what to do with natural materials.

- spend less and less time outside.

- have little opportunity any more to play freely in the natural outside world.

The woods are an absolutely ideal place for all senses. Here you will find sound, unknown and unusual smells, an inexhaustible variety of shapes and colours, an abundance of different materials and even –depending on the time of the year- fruits which you can collect and take home and eat. If we don't just regard the woods as a place for walking as many miles as possible, but rather for taking the time and trouble to discover and experience things, then it will acquire a totally new meaning for children and adults alike.

The children's senses are kept busy in the woods, but they are not over-stretched despite the range of things offered. They are attracted towards simple and natural things which calm them down rather wind them up!

WHAT ARE THEY LIKELY TO FIND AND EXPERIENCE?

The first walks you go on with children and for which you should take plenty of time, gives them the chance to:

- find their way around the area.
- investigate different sorts of ground.
- experience all sorts of smells.
- experience rustling leaves and the wind in the trees.
- listen to birds twittering and making knocking noises.
- find out about touching things like tree bark, branches and woodland fruits.
- become aware of the variety of different leaves.
- find the tracks of animals and people.
- watch beetles, snails, rabbits, etc.
- collect "valuable treasures".
- build little houses out of wood, leaves, branches and twigs.
- use tree trunks for balancing along.
- notice different kinds of light patterns.
- see and get to know the forest during the different seasons.

You can't get away without rules

To avoid certain risks and learn to treat nature properly, certain conditions must be fulfilled and important rules discussed with the children.

For group leaders and supervisors:

! The group must be accompanied by at least 2 adults, who have access to a mobile phone to call for help if needed.

! You'll need a first-aid kit.

! The area of woodland to be visited must be chosen carefully, marked off and be familiar to the accompanying adults.

! It should offer the children ample opportunity for collecting impressions and experience.

! Practical clothing and sensible shoes for all concerned are essential. (Don't forget rainwear!)

! A small wagon would help carry equipment and clothing.

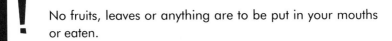

For the children:

Nobody must go out of hailing distance from the group.

It's a good idea to agree on some kind of sound for getting everyone together, e.g. a whistle, a particular call, a rattle…

! No fruits, leaves or anything are to be put in your mouths or eaten.

! No plants are to be torn out of the ground or damaged.

! Treat small animals with care and respect.

! Don't leave any rubbish lying on the ground in the woods.

WOODLAND DETECTIVES

After a few afternoons playing in the fresh air, we're now going to do something special. We'll become "chief snuffle noses" because we're going to train to be "woodland detectives".

The preparations are very easy:

1. Choose a suitable terrain and decide as to where certain tasks are best carried out.

2. Copy enough of the woodland-detective certificates, i.e. one per child.

3. Choose an appropriate stamp for the certificates, at best with a woodland motif.

4. Collect together all the necessary materials listed at the end of our range of tasks.

Right – and now there's nothing else to stop our big examination. Before we set out, let's get the children in the right mood:

"We all know that detectives are a particular cunning sort of people because they're good at watching and especially good at tracking down objects. But before you are a fully qualified 'woodland detective' with a special permit, you need to pass a few difficult exams. On our way through the forest, we shall pass a few special places where each of you can try out your special snuffle nose. It's best to work in pairs during such exciting assignments, so that you can take care of each other.

LOOKING

"Look for something soft nearby and bring it back here, so that we can put it on our woodland tablecloth."
As each group returns, they get another task:

- something smooth

- something hard

- something round

- something rough

- something which can make a noise

- something which you particularly like

EQUIPMENT: a white or uniformly-coloured tablecloth.

OBSERVING

"There are five objects under this cloth which you can also find around here. I'll lift the cloth up for a minute; have a good look and try to remember what you've seen. Go and look for the same things and bring them back here."

EQUIPMENT: Your choice of objects is determined by what you can find nearby e.g. pine cones, beech nuts, stones, little sticks, leaves, grass, etc.

FEELING AND RECOGNIZING

"In a wooded area where there are a lot of big trees, tell each other in turn about the tree:

One of you is blindfolded and is led by your partner to a tree. Without seeing it, you learn about the tree.

What does it smell like? What does it's bark fell like? How thick is it's trunk? Has it got moss on it? Can you feel any little twiglets or bumps? When you've felt everything, your partner brings you back again.

Then you can look around and see if you recognize your tree anywhere. Then swap roles!"

SMELLING

"Each of you chooses one of these little pots. Open the lid a bit and have a smell inside (you're not allowed to look inside). Now have a look around here and see if you can find something that smells like your pot. Bring it back here so that we can check it.

Another tip: if you rub a leaf or a plant between your fingers, the smell gets stronger."

EQUIPMENT: a little film pot with some crumpled fern leaves, pine needles, moss or woodland earth or some strong-smelling plant, e.g. wild garlic.

 ## DISCOVERING

"There are some strange things hidden around here. Go and look for things which don't belong in the forest, but please leave them where they are, so that other children can also look for them. Notice as much as possible and then tell me what you've found."

EQUIPMENT: things you wouldn't find in a wood like lettuce, a hard-boiled egg, a cuddly toy, an onion, a big potato, a banana, an apple tied to a branch, a wooden spoon stuck into the ground, etc. (about 10 objects).

STALKING

"You need to creep along through the woods, so that you don't frighten the animals away. Go as quickly as you can along this path and give yourselves plenty of time. Try to avoid rustling leaves or cracking branches."

 ## LISTEN CAREFULLY

This is a job that all would – be woodland detectives can do together:

"This is where we want to get to know the woodland sounds. Settle yourselves comfortably on the ground and shut your eyes. After a little while, when all the children are quiet, we'll try and hear lots of different sounds. Hold out your fist and put a finger out for each new sound you hear. Listen for birds twittering, rustling leaves, creaking branches, aeroplane noises and all sorts of other things as well. Remember what you've heard because I'm looking forward to what we'll tell each other later. Please, keep very, very still."

ANTS

The group has undoubtedly absorbed all sorts of noises and now we come to the climax. Everyone stands up and the group leader makes a ceremonial speech.

Now that you have successfully completed 7 woodland tasks, I solemnly pronounce you from today

A fully-fledged woodland detective.

Come up onto this tree stump one at a time or stand under this tree and touch the bark with your bottom (hand, tummy....)

We present you ...(name)... with this certificate with its official woodland animals stamp.

Congratulations!

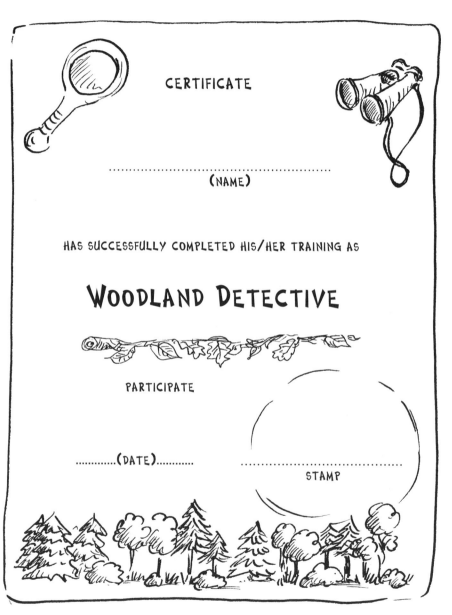

CERTIFICATE

....
(NAME)

HAS SUCCESSFULLY COMPLETED HIS/HER TRAINING AS

WOODLAND DETECTIVE

PARTICIPATE

.........(DATE)...........

....
STAMP

LET'S BUILD A HOUSE IN THE WOODS

Well-equipped for all weathers as usual (see p. 73), the little explorers start off on their walk through the woods. They've got a trailer with a sheet of plastic, rope, string, "woodland seats" and some fruit in it, in case they're hungry.

Where?

They look for a suitable building site.

> Take notice of the children's suggestions **!**

How big?

Everyone stands next to each other on the chosen site to see how big the house needs to be for everyone to fit inside. Or should we build 2 small houses?

> Wait for the majority decision **!**

What's needed?

We rub our hands together before setting to work to collect twigs, branches, tree trunks etc.

Twigs and branches ➡ the children can either carry on their own or help each other.

Larger branches ➡ are dragged and pulled along or fetched with ropes.

Tree trunks ➡ are either rolled or carried together.

> The children learn about group work with a feeling of togetherness, having respect for each other, helping one another and gaining a sense of achievement.

How shall we build?

The building materials are sorted out according to their function: Big and heavy tree trunks are put at the bottom, others put on top or upright against a tree, whilst smaller branches and twigs are woven together. You can also create windows and doors.

Try out ways of working together, also changing your plans and experimenting with something new – then you'll feel successful

!

The roof!

Once the house is standing firmly, the large sheet of plastic (or bedding sheet or parachute), which you've brought with you, can be spread out over the house or maybe fixed to the tree.

Things not belonging to the wood must be taken home again!

We can move in!

The tension is mounting. Will we all fit in? Can we take our "woodland seats" in with us? How can we make a table?

"Woodland seats" ➤ rubber mats cut to fit each little bottom.
"Woodland house table" ➤ is made out of moss in the middle.

We settle in and make ourselves really snug

Time for a break!

The well-known snack of apples and carrots appeals to everyone. Each child helps themselves to a certain agreed number of pieces of apple and carrot, e.g. 3 of one sort and 2 of another. If anyone counts wrongly, they give a piece to someone else.

Hurrah – I can already count

Games in the house

Can you hear how quiet it is?

Everyone sits in the house, shuts their eyes and listens. After a while they discuss what they've heard.

Now listen again ever more carefully!

Everyone shuts their eyes again and listens. The group leader asks all the children who've heard a bird to put their hands up. Then – whoever has heard the wind or a raindrop to put their hand up. Anyone who's heard a sound not belonging to the forest puts up both hands.

A leaf flutters by!

The group leader touches each child (with their eyes still shut) somewhere on their body. The child then names that part of the body.

The senses are sharpened and body awareness increased

You can still build or play outside the house, but soon we're going to have to say, "goodbye". Everything which doesn't belong to the wood is collected up, the roof taken apart and we take one last look at our "woodland house".

Before we go, we vow never to destroy our house, and lots of the children agree to come again from time to time with their families and check that everything's all right.

Will we go into the woods again for our next gymnastics session?

Who knows?!

An Invitation

We're looking for some treasure!

Meeting point: ....

Date: ....

Time: ....

Place: ....

Please bring weatherproof clothing and something to keep you going on our march.

Yours, ...

When we've found the treasure, we'll be back at about........

copy model

THE LONG-LOST TREASURE

No reward, without a bit of sweat! That means that we've a lot of preparing to do.

1. CHOICE OF TERRAIN:

A vital prerequisite for going on a "walk with a purpose" is to know your surroundings. If you, as exercise leader, are not very good at orienteering, then you'll need to mark out your intended route with little visible markers. It's not just enough to notice a particular tree or the type of path, because there might be a lot like that in the area!

When you've found a suitable area, you then need to think about how long your route can be, taking the shortest little legs in the group as a guideline. You also need to calculate time for discovering and experimenting, because the object of the exercise is not to charge through the woods and cover a high mileage! Obviously, the needs of the children must be taken into consideration and their wishes should be put first.

2. GETTING HOLD OF AND PREPARING YOUR EQUIPMENT:

The treasure we're looking for on our walk through the woods is obviously in a treasure chest. To make it even more exciting, this needs to be tied up with chains and padlocked in several places. Padlocks are particularly fascinating for children, and it would be good if you could arrange as many padlocks as the children who are participating. You can find them quite cheaply in toyshops.

All the keys can have a label attached to them by a bit of string, and the same label needs to be put on each padlock. Make sure your treasure looks like treasure, e.g. gold money chocolates, fruit or sweets wrapped in gold and silver paper; this all adds to the excitement.

The letter to the treasure-seekers needs photocopying with one treasure map per child.

3. SAFETY:

It goes without saying that you'll need more than one adult to accompany such a group of children into the woods, and this could easily be a mother or a father. You mustn't forget a mobile phone, plasters and bandages, paper tissues and toilet papers.

You'll also find useful a small wagon for rainwear, picnic food, etc.

4. THE TREASURE MAP:

All proper treasure hunts definitely need a treasure map. The older the little treasure seekers are, the more detailed the map. Then the children can read the marked points off the map and transfer them to their surroundings. A particular big tree, a bridge, fences, clearings, felled tree trunks are all fixed points which can be incorporated into your map with the minimum of artistic talent. A few secret signs and some special treasure hunt paper (like imitated parchment) will increase the children's excitement.

5. PREPARING THE WAY:

It's a good idea to keep on putting secret markers along the path to make the treasure seekers' route as varied as possible. To wind the children up and increase their excitement, you could use a few bits of material, an old shoe, socks with holes in, a squashed old hat, a singed bit of paper with secret hieroglyphics on it, some children's binoculars, an old leather glove, etc.

The little keys decorate bushes along the path which we recommend are not too far away from the place where the treasure chest has been hidden. Each child may then take a set of keys. A letter hidden there explains what the keys mean.

Hello, treasure seekers and adventurers!

I, the owner of the mysterious treasure, which I have hidden here in the forest, need to make all those who seek it aware of the following:

Waiting to be discovered by clever and crafty little people, my treasure chest has been made secure with a length of chain, 5 metres long, and lots and lots of padlocks. The treasure chest itself can only be opened when all the padlocks are unlocked. So, it is very, very important that nobody loses their key. Otherwise…

A tip from me: take good care of your keys, and all that remains for me to do is to wish you lots of luck as you go off looking.

6. THE SEARCH BEGINS:

All the preparations are now complete; the day for the Treasure Hunt has dawned and all the children are standing expectantly in front of us. We prepare them for this afternoon by first reading a story underlined with a tip from the newspaper, which we've brought with us:

Recently, I found an exciting story in the newspaper with an article about some missing treasure.

> Ninety-eight years ago, a strange, old man hid all his wealth and everything he possessed in our forest. Nobody mentioned anything about it for a long time, but now his grandchild has just got in touch with us from far away and said that whoever finds the treasure can keep it! We're talking about a box tied up with a heavy chain, and then firmly secured with the same number of padlocks, as there are children here.
>
> As you may well imagine, to open all these padlocks, you'll need exactly that number of keys hidden all around. You've got a treasure map to help you with your search. As soon as I read this story in the newspaper, the idea came into my mind of looking for the lost treasure together with you all, and that's why I've invited you onto this expedition today.

Because you never know what might happen during such a search, and because we need to read all the clues, I must ask you to stay close to me and watch carefully for all the obvious as well as hidden clues, as we go through the forest. Well, that's all I need to tell you for the moment, so we can set off.

But, hang on a minute, here's the treasure map from the newspaper with enough copies for all of you.

7. FINALE:

Tired but happy, we hope that everyone arrives back at the start safe and sound to be met by their parents.

To bake breadsticks

INGREDIENTS: a large lump of prepared yeast dough.

A fire is made in a safe place (barbecue stand, area of asphalt et.) out of pre-gathered dry wood. Each child then finds a long, firm stick (about 60-80 cm) made pointed at the end by an adult. When the fire is aglow, each child gets a ball of dough, rolls it into a long sausage shape with their hands and skewers it onto the end of the stick, winding the "tail" round the stick. The dough is then held over the fire and turned round and round until it is done.

The children will undoubtedly remember this exciting Treasure Hunt for a long time to come, especially the moment when they can pack important things into their own treasure chests locked with their own padlocks, which they can then take home with them.

LET'S MOVE
and Play...

Enjoyable Physical Activities and Games for Children between the Ages of 3 and 7

Each Volume:

Heidi Lindner (Ed.)
96 pages, Two-colour print, Numerous drawings
Paperback, 14.8 x 21 cm
c. £ 8.95 UK/$ 12.95 US/$ 19.95 CDN

Let's Move
Volume 1
Heidi Lindner (Ed.)
Great Games
for Small Children

ISBN 1-84126-064-9

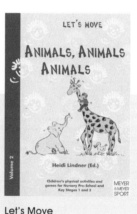

Let's Move
Volume 2
Heidi Lindner (Ed.)
Animals, Animals, Animals

ISBN 1-84126-065-7

Let's Move
Volume 4
Heidi Lindner (Ed.)
Wintertime

ISBN 1-84126-067-3

If you are interested in **Meyer & Meyer Sport** and our large programme, please visit us **online** or call our **Hotline!**

▶ online: www.meyer-meyer-sports.com
▶ Hotline: **++49 (0)1 80 - 5 10 11 15**
We are looking forward to your call!

Please order our catalogue!

MEYER & MEYER SPORT

MEYER & MEYER Verlag | Von-Coels-Straße 390 | D-52080 Aachen, Germany | Fax ++49 (0)2 41 - 9 58 10-10

Z08JJ/A12 08/01